Food

Beef stew

Biryani

Bread

Chapati

Cheese

Chicken curry

Chicken

Chocolate

Coffee

Couscous

Dessert

Falafel

Fish and chips

Fish

Fried chicken

Fried egg

Fried rice

Fries

Fruit juice

Goat meat

Hamburgers

Hummus

ice cream

Injera

Kebab

Lamb curry

Lasagna

Milk

Milkshakes

Pancake

Pizza

Porridge

Ribeye steak

Salad

Salmon

Samosa

Sausage

Shakshuka

Shawarma

Shrimp

Soup

Sphagetti

Sushi

Tacos

Tea

Ugali

Vegetable

Yoghurt